Family Walks
in the Peak District

by
Astrid and Ray Russell

20 circular walks of around three miles in length intended to be enjoyable and instructive to walkers of all ages.

DALESMAN BOOKS
1988

The Dalesman Publishing Company Ltd.,
Clapham, via Lancaster, LA2 8EB.

First published 1988
© Astrid & Ray Russell, 1988

ISBN: 0 85206 932 5

Another Dalesman book by the same authors:
Walks From Your Car . . . North East Derbyshire

Printed by Fretwell & Cox Ltd.,
Goulbourne Street, Keighley, West Yorkshire BD21 1PZ.

Contents

An Introduction   4
Places of Interest   5
─Abney and Stoke Ford   8
Alport and Youlgreave 10
Bakewell, Ashford-in-the-Water and the River Wye . . 12
Bonsall and Uppertown 14
─ Calver, Froggatt and the River Derwent 17
─ Castleton . . . . ─ 19
Chatsworth Park 21
Cromford Canal 23
Derwent and Ladybower Reservoirs 26
Elton and Harthill Moor 29
Flash and Three Shires Head 32
Hartington 34
Hathersage 38
Hathersage Moor 40
Monsal Dale 43
─ Over Haddon and Lathkill Dale 45
Stanton Moor 48
─ Tissington . . . . ─ 50
Win Hill 19
─ Wormhill and Peter Dale 20

Walks 9, 11 and 19 are rather more strenuous and less capable walkers should allow more time than usual to complete them.

Maps in the text by the authors.
Drawings by Alison and Helena Russell.

An Introduction

THE DERBYSHIRE PEAK DISTRICT is an area of interesting scenic and historic variation. There is a contrast between the heather-covered gritstone moorlands and edges and the gentler limestone country with its patchwork of grey walls and bright green fields crossed by sudden dramatic dales. The region contains much evidence of our ancestors' occupation and use of the land from early times. Prehistoric burial mounds, lead mining remains, early churches, great houses, picturesque villages and small bustling towns all provide a wealth of interest.

Over the past fifteen years we have walked and explored the area, sometimes taking longer and more strenuous walks on our own, but often in the company of children on shorter and less demanding routes planned to be enjoyable, interesting and instructive to them as well as us. This is a collection of some of those walks chosen to give a full flavour of the Derbyshire Peak District. The walks are of around three miles in length and while they will provide an enjoyable experience of the area for all walkers they are particularly suitable for groups which include children.

We have included details of some of the local events of the region and of places of interest that are close to particular walks. Visits to these, we feel, might be combined with appropriate walks to make a longer outing or provide interest should the weather turn unsuitable for walking.

All of the routes described are circular and most include some field footpath walking, some rough lane walking and the occasional stretch of walking on quiet roads. Most walks, especially in the winter, have wet and muddy patches so walking boots or wellies are essential footwear. All the paths have been recently walked and should therefore be followed without difficulty. However if you come across an obstruction to the right of way you are following do bring it to the attention of the local council which has the right by law to take responsibility for clearing the obstruction if, as occasionally happens, the landowner cannot be persuaded to do it.

Exploring this area has given us much pleasure — we hope this book helps to bring you similar enjoyment.

Maps
It is intended that all the walks can be followed by even the most novice walker from the description given. However, use of the appropriate Ordnance Survey map will provide additional help and

information. Maps particularly useful with this book are:
Ordnance Survey Map 'The Dark Peak' (Outdoor Leisure Series)
Ordnance Survey Map 'The White Peak' (Outdoor Leisure Series)

On any walk please observe the Country Code.

Places of Interest

* indicates a place which can be visited in any weather.
† indicates a place which makes an entry charge.
Unless otherwise stated places are open all the year round.

† **Arbor Low** (near Monyash): prehistoric ceremonial site known as the 'Stonehenge of the North'.
Ashbourne
A pleasant market town with interesting buildings. Market on Thursday and Saturday.
* St. Oswald's Church: of early English style with interesting monuments and impressive stained glass.
†* Indoor swimming pool.

Ashford-in-the-Water
* The Church of the Holy Trinity: an interesting early church restored in Victorian times but still containing Norman carving above the door. Also contains examples of the former local Black Marble industry and several funeral garlands.
The Sheepwash Bridge: a unique medieval bridge.

Bakewell
* The Original Bakewell Pudding Shop: a baker's shop where the famous Bakewell Pudding is still made to the original recipe.
* The Information Centre: based in the 17th century Market House and containing an interesting local exhibition.
The River Wye (below Bakewell Bridge): an ideal stretch of the river for trout spotting and duck feeding.
†* Old House Museum: Tudor house with displays illustrating 19th century life. Open April-October.
* All Saint's Church: impressive largely 13th century building with ancient stone cross and stone coffins.

Baslow
* St. Ann's Church.
17th century bridge with Watchman's Hut.

Buxton
Spa town with Roman origins and fine Georgian architecture.
†* Buxton Steam Centre: steam train exhibition with train rides available from April-November.
* Museum and Art Gallery: 'Story of the Peak' exhibition.
†* Poole's Cavern: cave at source of Wye with stalactites and stalagmites. Open Easter-November.
Solomon's Temple.

Castleton
* St. Edmund's Church: Norman chancel arch and 17th century box pews.
† Peveril Castle: small Norman keep.

†* Village Museum: open several afternoons a week Easter week and May-September.
†* Cavendish House Museum: large collection of Blue John including 100-year-old table.
†* Blue John Cavern: open daily but weekends only January and February.
†* Treak Cliff Cavern.
†* Speedwell Cavern: visitors travel underground by boat.
†* Peak Cavern: natural cave. Summer opening only.

†* **Caudwell's Mill** (Rowsley Village): a 100-year-old flour mill powered by water turbines. Also craft workshops. Open weekends and daily during August.
†* **Chatsworth Farm and Adventure Playground:** open Easter-October.
  * **Chatsworth Farm Shop** (Pilsley).
  * **Chatsworth Garden Centre** (Beeley): more than just a garden centre with something for most tastes.
†* **Chatsworth House and Gardens:** home of the Duke of Devonshire. Open Easter-October.
†* **Crich National Tramway Museum:** rides on vintage trams plus displays and exhibitions. Open most days April-September, some weekends October-December.

Cromford
Interesting village with many houses built by Arkwright to house employees. Large millpond.
†* Arkwright's Mill: first successful water powered cotton spinning mill. Exhibition and shop.
  * Scarthin Bookshop.
  * **Derbyshire Craft Centre** (Calver).

Eyem
A former lead mining village devastated by the plague in 1665.
  * St. Lawrence's Church: mainly 13th to 15th century but with Norman font, Celtic cross, sundial and other notable features.
Village stocks and bullring.
'Plague cottages' and 'plague graves' around village.
  * **Fairholme Information Centre:** display relating to building of reservoirs and 'Dam Busters' connection.
Foolow: outstandingly attractive hamlet.
†* **Good Luck Lead Mine** (Via Gellia, Cromford): 'working' example of mid-19th century mine. Open 1st Sunday in month.
†* **Haddon Hall:** a medieval manor house in a delightful setting. Open April-September
Hartington
Popular village with central pond.
  * St. Giles' Church: unusual 13th century effigy of lady under 'blanket'.
  * Hartington Cheese Shop.
  * Hartington Pottery: specialising in terracotta garden ware.
Hathersage
  * St. Michael's Church: contains stained glass from submerged Derwent Church. Little John's Grave in churchyard.
† Open air swimming pool: open summer months.
†* **High Peak Workshops** (near Cromford): restored workshops of High Peak Railway with exhibition and model shop. Open every weekend and mid week during school and Bank Holidays.
Hope
  * St. Peter's Church.

Ladybower Dam: largest and latest of the Derwent Valley reservoirs. Fine scenery.

† **Lea Gardens** (near Matlock): rhododendrons and azaleas. Open late March and July.
†* **Leawood Pump House:** restored 19th century steam engine. In steam several weekends between April and September.
* **Longshaw Lodge** (near Hathersage): National Trust Visitors' Centre in former shooting lodge. Open April-December.
Magpie Mine (Sheldon): former lead mine. Site can be visited any time.

Matlock Bath
† Heights of Abraham and Cable Car. Open Easter-October.
† High Tor: woodland walks, caves and playground.
† Gulliver's Kingdom: various 'theme' attractions. Open daily Easter-September plus some other weekends.
†* Aquarium: original thermal pool. Tropical and freshwater fish. Open Easter-September plus some other weekends.
†* Peak District Mining Museum and Temple Mine.
†* Indoor swimming pool at nearby Matlock.

Memorial to dog 'Tip' (near the western end of the Derwent Dam): immortalising a faithful dog whose master had perished on the moors.
†* **Middleton Top Engine House** (near Middleton-by-Wirksworth): stationary steam engine and visitors' centre. Engine open on Sundays and in steam on the first Saturday in the month. Visitors' centre open more frequently.
* **Monsal Head Craft Centre.**
* **Padley Chapel** (near Grindleford): 15th century chapel formerly attached to manor house. Annual pilgrimage held in memory of two martyred priests.
†* **Red House Stables** (Darley Dale): collection of horse-drawn vehicles and equipment.
† **Riber Wildlife Park** (Matlock): British and European birds and animals. Collection of vintage motorcycles.
Rowtor Rocks (behind Druids Inn at Birchover): range of gritstone rocks with several rocking stones and some carved into seats.

Tideswell
Large village formerly important market town with coaching inn.
* Church of St. John the Baptist: impressive and known as 'the Cathedral of the Peak'.
* Rock Shop: wide range of geological samples.
Welyarde Garden: beautifully maintained cottage garden. Open in Well Dressing Week and on several other weekends.
* **Tissington Church** (St. Mary's): many Norman features and monuments to the Fitzherbert family of the nearby Hall.

Winster
Many interesting buildings reflecting its former importance as centre of lead mining.
* National Trust Infomation Centre in 17th century Market House.
* **Youlgreave Church** (All Saints'): one of the most impressive churches in Derbyshire. Several fine monuments and very unusual 11th century font.

To obtain up-to-date opening times or precise dates of annual events contact any of the following Information Centres if your local Centre cannot help.
Ashbourne Information Centre, Market Place, Ashbourne. (0335) 43666.
Bakewell Information Centre, The Old Market House, Bakewell. (062981) 3227.
Buxton Information Centre, The Crescent, Buxton. (0298) 5106.
Castleton Information Centre, Castleton. (0433) 20679.
Chesterfield Information Centre, The Peacock Heritage Centre, Chesterfield. (0246) 207777.
Matlock Information Centre, The Pavilion, Matlock Bath. (0629) 55028.
Sheffield Tourist Information Centre, Town Hall, Sheffield. (0742) 734760.

1. Abney and Stoke Ford

Abney and Bretton Cloughs, with their varied woodland and clear streams, have a peaceful, almost secretive air. This easy walk through these secluded little valleys follows well-established paths, some of them being important routes in former times.
Distance: Just under 3 miles (5 kms).
Parking: On the roadside at Abney. Map reference 199799.

LEAVE ABNEY in the direction of Great Hucklow, passing the village hall and a telephone box on your left. Where the road goes downhill turn left over a stile by a foot-path sign to Nether Bretton. The path goes down to cross a footbridge and then climbs to a ladder stile. Turn left over the stile and follow the fence for a while then keep straight on across a slight hollow and on to a farm track. Cross the track and climb the bank bearing left with a marshy spring on your right.

When Cockey Farm comes into view ahead aim towards the left-hand side of it, climbing a stile in the corner of the field near a hawthorn tree. Now follow the wall on your left to reach the farm track at the side of the farm. Cockey Farm was the birthplace of William Newton, a local 18th century mill owner and self-taught poet known as the 'Minstrel of the Peak'. At a time when children working in mills often suffered at the hands of mill owners he was noted for the relative kindness shown to apprentices at his mill at Cressbrook.

Keep to the track with the wall on your left until about halfway down the field you bear right to pass the corner of a wall on your left and reach a ladder stile. Go straight across the next field, through a gateway and then continue ahead to a stile over the wall on your left beside a spring. Beyond the stile the clear path descends through the bracken and bushes to the valley below. Cross the wooden bridge, a stile and then another bridge. Now follow the path up the opposite hill, ignoring a side path which crosses the small stream on your left. Immediately beyond a small birch tree and oak tree together, pass another small path on your left and continue a short distance to a footpath marker post. Don't follow the main path but turn left here, cross the tiny stream and go straight forward skirting some marshy ground on your left. Now bear slightly left to go through a broken-down wall and over another small stream.

Just beyond this, bear right along a grassy path which goes through two derelict walls and bears right to skirt marshy ground

8

A beautiful walk. last bit was very wet.
(called at Hathersage Church to see little John's grave)

ABNEY AND STOKE FORD

and pass between two old gate-posts. Can you spot an unusual route marker here which points in the direction from which you have just come? Now turn left and walk with the wall on your left around a small hill. The clear path goes straight ahead, climbing gradually through bracken until, entering some trees, it crosses the remains of a short wall and turns left to a stile over a fence. Climb the stile and turn left along an obvious path beside a fence on the left. The path is now well-worn and easily followed. After passing a patch of marshy ground it comes to open ground, passing to the left of a ruined building and crossing a stream via a built-up causeway. Further along, climb a stile beside a gate and continue forward, descending gradually to reach the junction of the Highlow and Bretton Brooks at Stoke Ford.

Cross the two bridges and turn left along the path leading into the trees and signposted to Abney. The way is now quite clear climbing gradually through the woods with the brook on the left. In autumn this area produces a wide variety of fungi, including the attractive but poisonous fly agaric. Near the end of the wood the path passes beside an iron gate and crosses several tiny streams to reach open ground. Keep straight ahead, crossing a wooden stile before climbing more steeply to an old gate. Beyond this a stony, often very wet, track leads up to the road at Abney.

Some local places of interest: Eyam; Foolow; Hathersage.

2. Alport and Youlgreave

A stroll beside the quiet River Bradford (with a place to paddle if you want to!) is followed by a short climb to the pleasant village of Youlgreave and a return along the lower reaches of the River Lathkill.
Distance: Just over 2 miles (3½ kms.)
Parking: Above the bridge over the River Lathkill at Alport. Map reference 220646.

WALK BACK to a gate on the right just before the bridge and go through the stile beside it, along a track signposted to Middleton-by-Youlgreave. Cross the River Bradford and follow the track, with the river on your right. At one point there are lead mining spoil heaps between the track and the river and across the river can be seen one of the mine entrances from which the spoil came. Continue past a pack-horse bridge. This bridge took an old route over the river and up the walled lane to Youlgreave.

A little further on, the track crosses the river and reaches a minor road. Cross this and go through a stile beside the gate opposite. This is a pleasant spot to paddle on a warm day! A short distance further along the valley bear right, climbing a surfaced path, which goes through a stile and becomes a lane between houses. While the climb is fairly steep it gives enjoyable views down to the river and over the rolling countryside beyond. Below a small open-air 'swimming pool' has been constructed in the river. When you reach a minor road beside a chapel, walk a little way to the right to join the main street of Youlgreave opposite the fine 17th century Old Hall.

Turn right again and walk through the village. On the right you pass the former Co-op shop, now a Youth Hostel, and opposite it a large circular water cistern, erected in 1829 to provide piped water to the village. On reaching the church, said to be one of the finest in Derbyshire and containing amongst other interesting features a unique font, turn left along Conksbury Lane. After a short distance go down a narrow lane on the right, marked as a no through road for

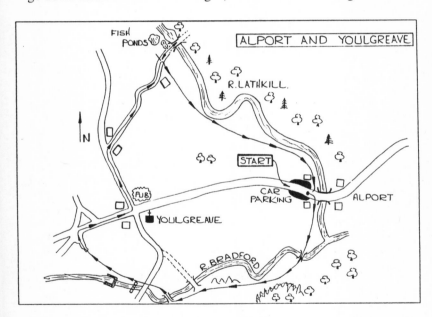

vehicles. This pleasant sheltered lane descends towards the River Lathkill. Shortly after passing an isolated house, the lane is crossed by a footpath. The route now goes through the stile on the right but before following it continue down to the little bridge over the river. This is known as Coal-pit Bridge from the days when coal from the Chesterfield area was carried this way by pack-horse. The river here is managed for fishing with recently restored fish-rearing ponds and a small fishing house.

Return to the stile and follow the obvious path across fields and through stiles to reach the road at Alport.

Some local places of interest: Arbor Low; Caudwell's Mill; Haddon Hall; Youlgreave Church.

3. Bakewell, Ashford-in-the-Water and the River Wye

A varied and scenic route linking a charming limestone village with an ancient market town.
Distance: Just under 4 miles (6kms).
Parking: In one of the car parks in Bakewell.

GO ALONG Bridge Street and cross Bakewell Bridge on the way out of town. Immediately over the bridge, go through an iron gate on the left and follow the path beside the River Wye. The path leads through a gate close to the river and then crosses a second meadow. Looking to the right from this path an 'ice-house' can be seen on the hillside above the modern houses. This small stone building is typical of those constructed for the preservation of food by wealthy households in the days before refrigeration. The path goes through a gate into a minor road. Turn left and walk along the road until you reach a narrow bridge on your left. The route now turns right uphill. However, before continuing, it is worth investigating the seventeenth century pack-horse bridge over the Wye. Pack-horses leaving town by the bridge would have continued on the uphill path which you are about to follow.

Continue uphill on the obvious path until a second gate is reached at the start of a walled track. Cross the stile beside the gate and immediately turn left into a field. Bear right across the field, passing a wall corner on your right, to reach a step stile into the next field. The view from this point is magnificent all round. Bear right and walk to the brow of the hill. When you see the roof of Cracknowl House ahead, aim for an iron gate in the wall to the right of the house. Bear left and after passing close to an evergreen plantation on your left continue in the same direction to a stile through the wall into a wood. Follow the obvious path close to the wall on your left

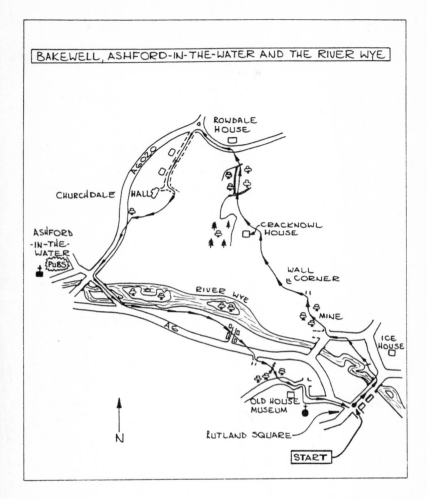

ROWDALE HOUSE

A6020

CHURCHDALE HALL

CRACKNOWL HOUSE

ASHFORD -IN-THE- WATER

PUBS

WALL CORNER

RIVER WYE

A6

MINE

ICE HOUSE

A6

OLD HOUSE MUSEUM

RUTLAND SQUARE

N

START

down through the wood, through a gate and across a field to reach the road opposite Rowdale House.

Turn left and walk a short way to a road junction. Here turn left up a tarmacked lane, signposted as a public footpath. Continue on until a point just before the lane goes through the gate leading to Churchdale Hall. Now turn left on to a track and then almost immediately turn right through a gate. Go straight ahead to reach a ladder stile between two lots of trees. Note the 'ha-ha' between the edge of this field and the garden of Churchdale Hall. This sort of sunken fence was constructed to deter livestock from entering the gardens of large houses without obstructing the view. Bear left to follow the path down the hill, over two more stiles, and, after crossing a small stream, climb through a finely decorated stone squeezer stile on to the main A6020 road. Turn left and walk down the road towards Ashford-in-the-Water.

Just before the road crosses the River Wye, the route turns to the left. However, before continuing, you may wish to visit Ashford which has several pleasant pubs and includes the Sheepwash Bridge and an interesting church among its attractions. The route now crosses two small bridges and then, immediately before the main road, turns left through a gate in the wall by a footpath sign to Bakewell. Continue beside the river along the obvious path which eventually leaves the river to bear right across a field and reach a narrow path between some houses. Cross the road and continue forward to cross a field and bear slightly right to a stile and on to the main A6 road.

Here, if you wish to return to Bakewell by the most direct route, turn left and follow the road back to Rutland Squàre in the centre of the town.

For a much pleasanter, though slightly more energetic, way back to Bakewell walk a few yards to the left then cross the road to where a rough track leaves it at the foot of a wooded slope. On the left at the start of this track a path climbs up the slope through the trees, levelling out at the top on to a school playing field. Bear left to cross the field diagonally, going through a line of bushes and small trees, and make for the furthest left of three large trees along the top side of the field. Here a footpath sign shows the way through the hedge on to a minor road. Turn left and follow the road downhill, passing close to the Old House Museum and Bakewell Church, and eventually reaching Rutland Square.

Some local places of interest: Ashford-in-the-Water; Bakewell; Chatsworth Estate; Caudwell's Mill; Haddon Hall; Magpie Mine.

4. **Bonsall and Upper Town**

A short easy route around a pleasant old leadmining village set in a peaceful valley.
Distance: Just under 2 miles (3½kms).
Parking: On the land immediately below the recreation ground at Bonsall. Map reference 280579.

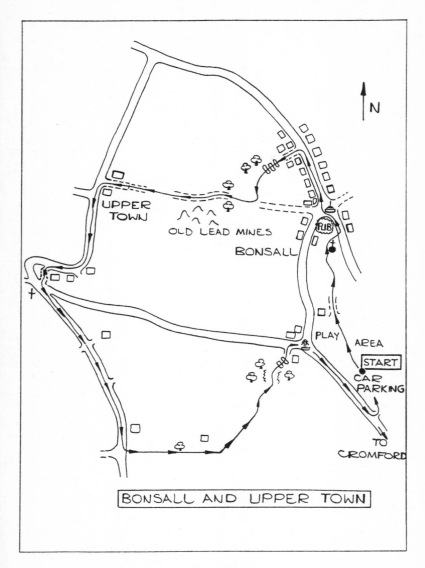

N

BONSALL AND UPPER TOWN

WALK up the recreation ground and climb the steps up the hillside
at the far right-hand corner, turning left along a level path to the
lower side of the churchyard. Turn right and walk through the
churchyard to the lych-gate which takes you into the road at the
other side. Turn left and walk down the road to the centre of the

village and the impressive Market Cross with its 13 steps. Bonsall is an ancient village, mentioned in the Domesday Book but now quiet and peaceful.

Walk to the right up the High Street passing a butcher's shop and the old Hall on the left. Look for a row of cottages on the left, at right angles to the road, at the far end of which can be seen a gate leading to some stone steps up a field. Climb the steps and keep straight on up the field, gradually getting closer to the wall on the left. When the wall turns sharply left, go through a stile in another wall ahead. Now ignore the stile opposite and bear right to another squeezer stile a little way up the field which brings you into a narrow surfaced track between walls. As you climb, a delightful view unfolds back over the village with its prominently sited church and in the far distance the 'cliffs' of Crich with Crich Stand on top. Over the wall on the left the disturbed ground shows the reason for Bonsall's prosperity in former times — lead mining. The hills around the village were full of small mines with tracks and paths linking them to the village and farms. Follow the track, keeping straight ahead through stiles where it opens out into fields, eventually passing between some houses and into the road at Upper Town.

Turn left and walk down the road. A little way past a right-hand bend, when the road begins to drop steeply into the dale, turn left down a steep little path which passes the end of some cottages and brings you to the road below, opposite a chapel. Cross the road and climb another road just to the left of the chapel. Continue forward, passing a cross-roads with a farm track then another track and a barn on the left. Not far beyond the barn, look for a stile on the left. Go through and keeping straight ahead cross four fields via stiles.

In the fifth field bear left to a stile beneath the overhead cables and continue to bear left to the next stile near a gateway. Now follow the wall and then the hedge on your right through two more stiles. Here the path drops steeply and turns sharply left, then bears right to another stile. This takes you down some steps and along a walled path to reach the road opposite the recreation ground.

Some local places of interest: Cromford; Crich National Tramway Museum; Good Luck Lead Mine; Lea Gardens; Matlock Bath; Middleton Top Engine House; Riber Wildlife Park.

5.   Calver, Froggatt and the River Derwent

(24·391)

A gentle stroll beside a beautiful stretch of the River Derwent.
Distance: Around 2½ miles (4kms).
Parking: On the roadside near the church and school at Calver.
    Map reference: 247744.

WALKING from the car towards Calver Bridge, turn right along the minor road signposted to Froggatt and Sheffield. The River Derwent runs alongside the road on the left. Across the river is Calver Mill, originally a cotton-spinning mill, whose gaunt appearance provided an ideal setting for the television series 'Colditz' about life in a German prison camp during the Second World War. When the wall on the left ends, cross the stile on to a clear path which follows the river closely to New Bridge. Shortly before reaching the bridge you pass the rather dilapidated weir which was constructed to provide a head of water to power the original water-driven machinery of Calver Mill. Later, as you return on the opposite side of the river, you will walk beside the 'goit' along which the water flowed to the mill.

Emerge on to the road at New Bridge and immediately opposite go through a gap in the wall and continue on the obvious path beside the river. Further along, approaching Froggatt Bridge, the banks of the river are particularly beautiful in springtime when coloured by frequent clumps of snowdrops and daffodils. Just before the bridge the path climbs to a stile in the wall and you emerge on to the road. Turn left along the road to reach the unusually shaped bridge.

Immediately over the bridge go through a stile on the left and on to a path below. The path now either continues straight ahead on the right of a small copse of conifer trees or to the left of the copse and close to the river bank. Various sorts of fir cones can be found here. The copse is also interesting in that it contains alder trees whose seed cones are used in the preparatory stage of well-dressing known as 'black-knobbing' which involves outlining the picture by pressing the cones into the clay. At the end of the copse the two paths join and continue alongside the river.

Just before reaching New Bridge the path bears right to cross Stoke Brook via a small wooden bridge and then returns towards the river and reaches the road through a stile beside the bridge. Go across the road and through the stile opposite to continue along the track which runs at first between some buildings and then close to

17

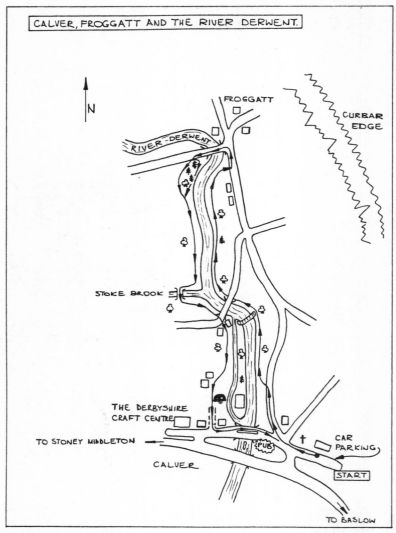

CALVER, FROGGATT AND THE RIVER DERWENT.

FROGGATT

CURBAR EDGE

RIVER DERWENT

STOKE BROOK

THE DERBYSHIRE CRAFT CENTRE

TO STONEY MIDDLETON

CALVER

PUB

CAR PARKING

START

TO BASLOW

the mill goit. Eventually the path bears right away from the goit and passes to the right of a small camping site. Continue along the obvious path back to the road at Calver. Turn left along the road and over Calver Bridge back to the starting point.

Some local places of interest: Baslow; Chatsworth Estate; Derbyshire Craft Centre; Eyam.

29.4.90 *3 hrs.*

A very hard walk.

6. Castleton

we nearly got lost a couple of times.

Castleton is a very interesting village both historically and geographically and thus is popular with walkers and other visitors to the Peak District. This low level walk follows some of the less frequented paths around the head of the valley giving wide views of the area and its notable features.
Distance: About 3 miles (5kms).
Parking: In the public car park at Castleton.

FOLLOW the footpath on the right-hand side of the car park beside a stream and go along a rough lane between cottages into Hollowford Lane. Here turn left, in the direction of Edale and Hollins Cross. Walk along the metalled road, over a stream, and continue to pass an unusual type of hay barn with the roof suspended on pulleys. The road gives glorious views to the Winnats Pass and Mam Tor on the left and to Back Tor on the right. Pass the Hollowford Outdoor Centre and shortly afterwards, where the road bends left, turn right along a rough track.

A little way along, go through a gate on the left and walk up the farm track. At the top of the field, where the track goes through a gateway, keep to the left of it to cross a small wooden bridge and

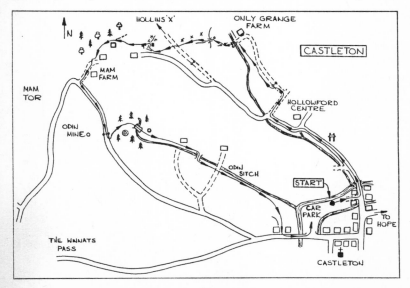

then a stile. Now go straight ahead crossing several stiles to reach a final stile, just to the right of where a stream comes through a wall, bringing you into a rough track by Only Grange Farm.

Here turn left, go through the metal gate and follow the track into a field with a wire fence on your right. Go through a gap between two large wooden posts in the fence and cross a small ditch via some stones. Now bear left and cross the field to reach a large stone post and a signpost to Back Tor beside a gap in the wall. Turn left and follow the clear path over a small stream. Almost immediately, when the path begins to descend alongside a hollow, look for a narrow grassy path leading off to the right. The path is narrow but clear through the bracken, keeping fairly level and roughly parallel to some overhead power lines on the right. It brings you to a wide path close by a wooden stile. This wide and well-worn path was part of the daily route taken by workers from Castleton to the cotton spinning mill at Edale in the next valley.

Climb the stile and almost immediately bear left along another narrow path. This path is not very obvious at first but becomes clearer, going downhill to meet a fence on the left beside a farm track. Ignore a stile over this fence and continue, bearing slightly right, climbing gradually to cross a tiny stream by a brick water tank. Keeping in roughly the same direction reach the corner of a wire fence on your left and follow it for a short distance, passing beneath an overhead power line and crossing two small streams. The path moves away from the fence and bears right around a slight hollow in which there is a stile over a wall.

Don't descend to the stile but keep bearing right, cross another stream then keep straight on past a large tree on your left to climb two stiles close together. Shortly after this the path is joined by a wider path coming down the hill on the right and passes just above a clump of trees behind a house on the left. Climb a stile just before a National Trust signboard and follow the marker posts to a fence where the path turns right to cross a stile on to a rough lane.

Turn right and follow the lane behind Mam Farm and on to the abandoned section of the A619 road below Mam Tor. In 1802 when the Sheffield-Manchester Turnpike Trust routed their new road around the shoulder of Mam Tor (the 'Shivering Mountain'), instead of up the steep and narrow Winnats Pass, they did not take into account the unstable nature of the ground in this area. Extensive landslips occurred, particularly after periods of heavy rainfall, causing the eventual permanent closure of the road in 1977. Turn left and walk down the road, passing on your right one of the cast iron mile-posts set up by the Turnpike Trust. Go through a gate near which, to the right of the road, is the entrance to the old Odin leadmine. This mine is thought to date back to Celtic times and produced lead ore until its closure in the late 19th century. A little further on, a footpath on the left of the road takes you over a stile to the remains of the ore crushing circle. When lead ore had been taken from the ground it needed to be crushed into smaller pieces and this gritstone wheel with its iron tyre, introduced around 1820, did the job for the Odin mine.

Continue along the path, over a stream and across spoil heaps, passing another shaft on your left and then going down through bushes to Knowlgate Farm. Now go straight ahead through a squeezer stile, with the stream known as the Odin Sitch on your right. Shortly after another stile the path crosses the stream and continues along the other side until a stile takes you on to a farm track. Go through a stile almost opposite and follow the clear path across the fields. After a squeezer stile beside some trees the path follows a wall, later a fence, on the right and eventually emerges into the main road at Castleton via a narrow walled 'gennel'. Turn left and walk back to the car park.

Some local places of interest: Castleton village.

7. Chatsworth Park

The park surrounding Chatsworth House is justifiably popular. This easy route is not much frequented yet gives outstanding views of Chatsworth and the surrounding area.
Distance: Just over 3½ miles (5¾kms).
Parking: In the car park at Calton Lees (near Chatsworth Garden Centre). Map reference 258685.

FROM the car park, walk along the metalled lane beyond the entrance to the Garden Centre, past the estate sawmill on the left, to reach Calton Lees. Here the lane bends sharply left but you continue straight ahead through a gateway and along an unsurfaced track. There is a hedge on the left, and later a wall, with a stream beyond it. On the hillside to the right of the track there are often pheasants and rabbits to be seen.

Approaching Calton Houses, the track climbs sharply to the right and then to the left before passing between the buildings. At this point there is a magnificent view back towards Beeley Moor. The path becomes narrower and runs between walls, turning to the right and through a gate into an open field. Now continue up the hill, keeping to the wall on the right until at the top the path bears left away from the wall and makes towards an evergreen plantation opposite. While crossing the large field, you pass a footpath sign on the left indicating a way to Ballcross and Bakewell. The unusual house seen on the right is known as Russian Cottage, as a consequence of the 6th Duke's friendship with a Czar.

At the far side of the field, a stile beside a gate leads into a track and down through New Piece Wood. Climbing over the step stile at the bottom of the wood reveals a wonderful panorama of Chatsworth and its setting. Go forward down the hill, passing first a small plantation and then a larger, older one on your right. Make straight ahead towards the spire of Edensor church. The park's herd of deer is often seen in this area.

As you approach Edensor church, look for a small metal gate, above a few steps, a little to the left of the churchyard. This takes you down some steps between the houses and out into the village street of Edensor. Until 1839 Edensor village stood on the opposite side of the road which runs through the park, and nearer to Chatsworth House. In a general re-designing of the surrounds of the house the 6th Duke, wishing to improve the view, had the village demolished and rebuilt, in a great variety of architectural styles, on

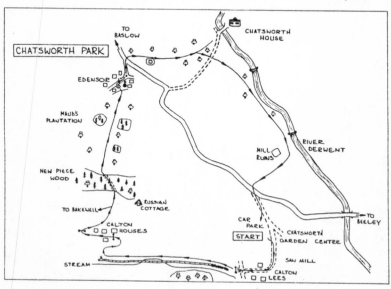

its present site. The church, added in 1867, contains evidence of the original Norman structure and an interesting monument to Henry and William Cavendish. Turn right and walk past the church, bearing left towards the gate which leads on to the road.

Cross the road and continue along a path beside a large tree with a seat around it. The house seen on the right is the only building remaining of the original village of Edensor. Where the path bends left, among some trees, bear right off it and aim straight downhill towards the river, crossing the driveway to Chatsworth House part way down. On reaching the river continue straight ahead along the obvious path beside it. The path moves away from the river slightly but returns to it near the old weir, just before the ruins of Chatsworth Mill. Beyond the mill turn right and climb the hill to a white gate on to the road. Cross the road and return to the car park.

Some local places of interest: Chatsworth Estate; Caudwell's Mill.

8.   Cromford Canal

The way in which different forms of transport over several centuries have used the same river valley is seen on this easy walk. On summer weekends you can complete the first part of the route by horse-drawn canal boat if you wish!
Distance: Just over 3 miles (5kms).
Parking: In the public car park at Cromford Wharf. Map reference 290570.

THE CROMFORD CANAL was opened in 1793 and linked the growing industries of the Derwent valley (in particular Richard Arkwright's mills at Cromford) with the Erewash Canal at Langley Mill and hence with the River Trent. From near Cromford a railway provided a link with the Peak Forest Canal at Peak Forest on the other side of the limestone plateau.

Walk along the tow-path beside the canal until you reach the workshops at High Peak Junction. Here a swing bridge crosses the canal leading to an Information Centre and picnic tables.

Continue with the water on your right, passing the Wharf Sheds on the opposite bank. Here goods were transferred between the railway and the canal. A short distance further along on the left you pass Leawood Pumphouse, with its distinctive chimney. The steam engine inside, dating from 1849, was used to raise water to the canal from the nearby River Derwent and can still be seen in steam on some summer weekends. Just beyond the pumphouse the canal crosses the River Derwent on an aqueduct.

At the end of the aqueduct the derelict Lea branch of the canal leads off to the left. Turn left along its tow-path. A short distance along, the path crosses a bridge over the railway (originally there was a cast-iron aqueduct here) and then continues beside the now dry and overgrown canal bed. In the trees and bushes along here we have seen treecreepers, long-tailed tits, bullfinches and other small birds. Just after passing a house on the left look for a narrow path which leads off to the left between walls. Turn down it and where it ends, beside a stream, turn right into a lane and walk a few yards between houses to emerge on to the road.

Turn right and walk a short distance up the road to where a lane goes off to the left just before the entrance to John Smedley's mill. At the start of the lane there is a stile through the wall on the left. Go through and follow the obvious path straight ahead and uphill through the trees. The path is quite clear through the woods and there are good views back across the valley to the canal. This part of the walk, until shortly before you rejoin the road near Cromford, follows the line of a pack-horse route from Cromford Bridge, a well-established highway before the turnpike road was built along the valley bottom.

CROMFORD CANAL

The path leaves the wood through a squeezer stile beside a gate and continues as a walled track, passing a cottage on the right, to reach a tarmacked road. Turn left and walk down the road. Beyond the driveway to Bow Wood Farm, on the left, the road passes between stone gate-posts. Shortly after this, look for a wooden stile over the fence on the right. Cross the stile and bear left over the field

LEAWOOD
PUMPHOUSE

to find a stone stile at the far corner. Bear left to the remains of another squeezer stile in a broken-down wall. Now follow the tracks worn into the hillside up the field, past a small, stone water trough on the right, and aim for a telegraph pole when it comes into view ahead. The stile is to the left of the pole. Continue forward beside a hedge on the left and soon, where the path turns slightly left and makes downhill towards a gate, leave the obvious track and bear right. Aim towards some wooden fencing about halfway up the field at the edge of the wood ahead. There is a stile at the side of the fence and a narrow path winds into the wood. It becomes wider and eventually crosses a stile into a field at the farther side of the wood.

Turn left and follow the clear path down the field and over a stile on to the road near Cromford station. Turn right and walk along the road to Cromford Bridge, just before which is the entrance to Willersley Castle, the mansion which Sir Richard Arkwright built for himself. The Saxon ford at Cromford was replaced by a medieval bridge, with a bridge chapel (where travellers could offer prayers for a safe journey) of which the remains can be seen at the farther end, beside the much later fishing lodge. An inscribed stone on the downstream parapet supposedly records an amazing escape from injury by a horse and rider who plunged from the bridge into the river in 1671.

Go over the bridge and a little way along the road is the entrance to the car park.

Some local places of interest: Cromford; Crich National Tramway Museum; Good Luck Lead Mine; High Peak Junction Workshops; Lea Gardens; Leawood Pump House; Matlock Bath; Middleton Top Engine House; Riber Wildlife Park.

9. Derwent and Ladybower Reservoirs

Beginning and ending with an easy stroll beside scenic reservoirs this walk also includes a steady climb to Pike Low, giving panoramic views of the hills and moorlands surrounding the upper Derwent Valley. Inexperienced walkers should only attempt this walk in clear summer weather.
Distance: Just over 3½ miles (5¾kms).
Parking: Fairholme car park near the Derwent Dam.
  Map reference 173893.

UNTIL the early 1900s the upper reaches of the River Derwent flowed through a secluded valley of scattered farms beneath the bleak moorlands. The need for increased water supplies to Sheffield, Derby, Nottingham and Leicester led to the building of the Howden and Derwent dams between 1901 and 1916. The larger Ladybower reservoir was constructed between 1935 and 1945 and this involved the flooding of two villages. The landscape was further changed by the large-scale planting of trees on the hillsides around the reservoirs.

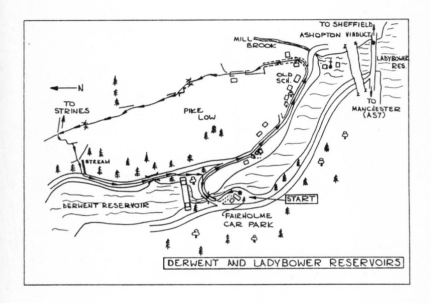

DERWENT AND LADYBOWER RESERVOIRS

Leave the car park, passing the Ranger's Office on your left and go along a footpath beside a wooden fence on your right. On reaching a metalled road turn right along it to cross the short stretch of the River Derwent which flows between the Derwent and Ladybower Reservoirs. The road passes the massive wall of the Derwent Dam on the left then bends right and climbs to level out with the Ladybower Reservoir on the right. Keep straight on passing a telephone box and Derwent Lodge, once an entrance to Derwent Hall, on your right. Further on, you pass several houses and the former Derwent school, complete with bell. Derwent was one of the villages flooded by the Ladybower Reservoir. Most of the buildings were demolished but the church spire was left intact for some years and could be seen when the water level was low.

27

However, when drought conditions tempted people to wade out to it, it was deemed unsafe and was blown up. Shortly after the school, just before the road begins to descend, turn left up a track to pass through a gateway then between two old farm buildings.

Keeping to this obvious track, climb gradually and cross several stiles to reach a gate beside a house. As you climb, wonderful views unfold of Derwent Edge and Back Tor over to the right and down Ladybower Reservoir to Ashopton Viaduct. Ashopton was the other village which disappeared beneath the water and the viaduct was built where the village used to be. Go through the gate and follow the track up the hill, ignoring a path to the right immediately beyond the gate. You reach a wall corner on your right then, following the direction of a footpath sign, bear right to a ladder stile. Now aim slightly left to follow the clear path. At a wall corner go through a broken-down wall and turn right to continue with the wall on your right.

The path is quite clear, alongside the wall, until on approaching a small plantation it bears left away from the wall as shown by a footpath sign. Shortly afterwards cross the remains of a wall then make for a ladder stile beside a gate which is visible on the skyline ahead. The path runs beside a wall on the left for a while before reaching the stile. Continue forward still on a clear path until you reach a green metal signpost, where two paths cross, showing the way to Strines via Bradfield Gate Head.

Here turn left down a narrow path which crosses a ruined wall. The path goes straight ahead for a little way then turns left and becomes level for a short distance before turning right again and going almost straight ahead down the hill. As you approach a wall above a wood the path becomes less clear but make your way to an open gateway where the wall meets another wall coming from the right. The path goes through the gateway and downhill to emerge on to the track beside the Derwent Reservoir. Turn left and walk along the track.

Just before you come level with the dam wall cross a stile over a fence on the right and follow the path down through the trees to the road beneath the dam. During World War II the Derwent and Howden dams were used as practice grounds for the development of the famous 'bouncing bomb' and, later, scenes from the 'Dambusters' film were shot there. Turn right and re-trace your steps to the car park.

Some local places of interest: Fairholme Information Centre; Hope; Memorial to dog 'Tip'.

10.   Elton and Harthill Moor

*Starting at the quiet village of Elton this walk gives wide views from
the fields of Harthill Moor and includes a site of geological and
historical interest, with the well-concealed home of a medieval
hermit.*
Distance: Just over 3 miles (5kms).
Parking: On the roadside near Elton church. Map reference 223609.

THE NEARNESS of the sturdy upland village of Elton to the
ancient British route known as the Portway — 'port' being the old
name for a market town — suggests that it is of very old foundation.

NINESTONES CIRCLE – HARTHILL MOOR

This ancient route was well established long before the Romans
occupied Britain and it continued to be a highway for centuries
afterwards. Part of this walk is along a section of the Portway.

   Walk a short distance down Well Street alongside the church and
bear left along a track signposted to Youlgreave. Where the track
turns right, go forward through a stile beside a gate. Turn
immediately left, go through a stile and then bear right down the

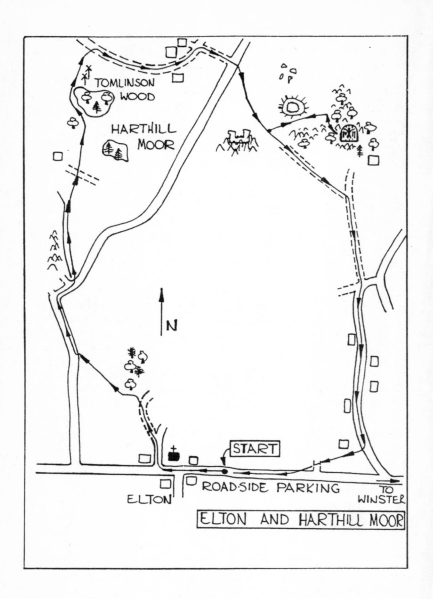

TOMLINSON WOOD

HARTHILL MOOR

N

START

ROAD-SIDE PARKING

ELTON

TO WINSTER

ELTON AND HARTHILL MOOR

next field. Go through a stile in the wall at the bottom (*not* the stile at the right-hand corner), continue in the same direction through the next stile then turn sharp left and into a minor road.

Turn right and walk up the road. At the third footpath sign on the left (signposted to Harthill Moor) go through a gateway and along the top of a field with a wall on your left. Where the wall swings away to the left continue straight forward, over a stile and into a large field. Continue straight ahead, passing the corner of a wall on your left, across a farm track then via two further stiles to the edge of Tomlinson Wood. Bear left around the edge of this plantation which contains a great variety of trees, home to many small birds.

On reaching another stile go forward, following the line of the overhead cables and skirting the corner of a wall on the left. A squeezer stile followed by a wooden stile brings you to a farm track. Turn right up the track in the direction shown for Stanton. At the top of the prominent hill on the left is Castle Ring, the site of an Iron Age fort. Follow the clear path past Harthill Moor Farm and on to the road.

Cross the road and go through the stile opposite to bear right across a field. As you cross the field look to your left to see the four remaining large stones of a Bronze Age stone circle, probably originally nine in number, and dating from between 1500 BC and 1000 BC. The clear path crosses two fields bringing you to the foot of Robin Hood's Stride. This rock formation is so called because the outlaw is supposed to have been able to step from one pinnacle to the other! Another name for it is Mock Beggars Hall — seen in silhouette from a distance the pile resembles the outline of a large turreted mansion. The route goes to the left around the base of Robin Hood's Stride. Before continuing down the track take the path through the wall on the left to cross rough grassland and reach a wooden stile. Climb the stile and a Hermit's Cave is hidden in the rocks below to the right. It contains an artistically carved crucifix, thought to have been fashioned about 1300.

Return to the main track, which was part of the Portway though the ancient road diverges slightly part way down and runs in the hollow on the right. Continue downhill to reach a minor road which you follow up the hill opposite, still on the line of the Portway. Eventually you reach a second footpath sign on the right, at a bend in the road and shortly before reaching the Winster-Elton road. Follow the footpath which runs above a modern house, through several stiles and on to the road leading back into Elton.

Some local places of interest: Red House Stables Carriage Museum; Rowtor Rocks; Winster.

11.   Flash and Three Shires Head

A slightly longer walk but worth the extra effort. The walk follows old paths through the secluded valleys around the meeting point of Derbyshire, Staffordshire and Cheshire. Allow time to take the uphill return slowly!
Distance: Just under 4 miles (6kms).
Parking: On the roadside at Flash. Map reference 026672.

THIS WALK starts from the tiny village of Flash, notable as the highest village in England — the sign on the Post Office recording its position as 1518 feet above sea level. It lies astride a watershed. On one side rise the rivers Dove and Manifold, the waters of which eventually flow into the North Sea via the Humber and on the other the River Dane starts — its eventual destination being the Irish Sea. Flash's other claim to fame is its association in former times with the coiners of counterfeit money — hence the term 'flash money'.

From the church at Flash, walk along the road which passes the pub on the left and then the former Wesleyan chapel on the right. Continue down the hill and just past a derelict barn in a field on the right look for a stile over the wall on the right. The worn stone of the stile suggests that this has been a much used route over many years. Almost immediately, cross another stile then bear slightly left down to a wooden stile over the boundary fence of a tarmacked driveway. Turn right and walk a short distance up the drive to cross another stile on the left. Go slightly right to the next stile and then straight ahead over two more. Now bear right, passing below a few bushes on your right to climb a stile over a fence and descend steeply to a foot-bridge. This is a crossroads of old routes, evident from the ford above the little waterfall.

Follow the clear path signposted to Drystone Edge. The stony track beside the stream gradually climbs to reach a level, surfaced lane. Turn left and walk along the lane. Pass through a gate just before a farm, beyond which the lane becomes rougher. A little further on ignore the track which goes left down a field and keep straight on along a walled path, passing an old building on your left. What was put into this building through the curious little opening low down in the wall? The clear path continues, sometimes walled only on one side, gradually descending towards the river on the left. Just after going through a gate the pack-horse bridge over the infant River Dane can be seen. Three Shires Head with its two bridges and waterfalls can be a tranquil and secluded spot. The pool below the bridge is called Panniers Pool from the trains of pack-horses which used this river crossing many years ago — the panniers were the large containers fastened on either side of the pack saddle.

Cross the first, smaller bridge, thus stepping into Derbyshire, then turn right through a gate and climb the stony track beside the stream on your right. When you reach a small stone bridge cross it, returning to Staffordshire, and follow a walled track uphill and around a left-hand bend to join a surfaced road beside a wooden gate near a derelict farm. Turn right and walk along the road, following it around a bend and down to a road junction. Here walk a short distance along the road to the left then cross a slab bridge over the small stream on the right.

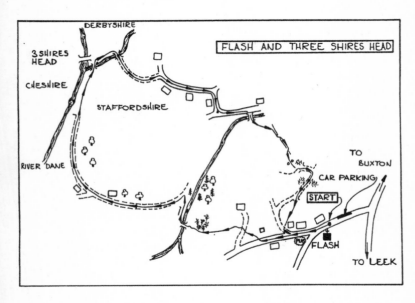

The path bears slightly to the left to reach a wall and then follows it up the hill. When you reach a stile over the wall cross it and continue uphill with the wall and a fence now on your right. Just before the top of the hill, climb a wooden stile over the wall on your right then bear left uphill to pass between the two wooden posts ahead. This hill is Wolf Edge — probably so named as being one of the last outposts of wolves in the area. If the weather is clear there are superb views from here over the hills towards Cheshire. The path is not clear now. Aim ahead but slightly left over the hilltop and down the other side, skirting some rocks on your left, to reach a gateway and a derelict stile at the start of a short walled track.

Go down the track, over a wooden barrier at the bottom and turn right to walk alongside a wall on your right. After passing through a gateway the path becomes walled on both sides. This last stretch can be very wet at times but it is possible to make slight detours around the worst sections of it. Where the track bears right keep straight ahead through a stile beside a gateway on the left of the track. Bear slightly left across a field to a step stile then go straight ahead, crossing another stile to reach a gate into a walled track, just beyond a building on the left. Turn left down the track to the road then left again along the road and back into Flash.

Some local places of interest: Buxton.

12.   Hartington

Starting from the attractive village of Hartington the first part of this walk crosses the quiet limestone-walled fields above the village. The latter part is through an understandably popular stretch of Dove Dale.
Distance: 3 miles (5kms).
Parking: In the village centre. Map reference 128605.

IN THE CENTRE of Hartington a signpost indicates the road to Ashbourne (B5054). Walk a few yards in the direction shown and turn right at the road junction just before a telephone box. Opposite the junction is the 150-year-old Market Hall with three unusual stone arches. A little way up the road at a sharp left-hand bend take the narrow footpath on the right alongside a cottage. On reaching a field turn left and keeping the wall on your left climb the field and pass through two stiles to reach the minor road above. Notice the squeezer stile leading on to the road — there are several finely-dressed stone squeezers of this unusual design in the locality.

Turn right and walk on the road to find a step stile over the wall on the left, signposted to Dale End. Cross the large field diagonally, bearing right. The next step stile over the wall on the opposite side of the field is rather derelict but its position is evident from a large stone in the grass beside the wall. Over the wall turn right and follow the track until it ends in a large field. Bear slightly right and cross the field to find another derelict stile a little to the left of a group of four large trees. Keeping in the same direction cross to the far right-hand

ABOVE HARTINGTON

corner of the next field where a footpath post marks the position of the stile.

Turn left along the lane for a short distance and look for a stile over the wall on the right. It is not very clear but is sited just before the second of the field walls which run at right-angles to the lane.

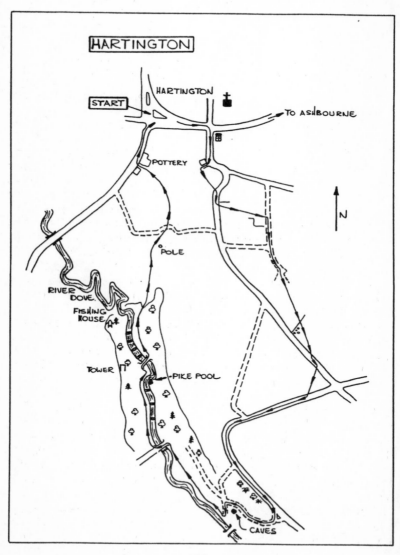

Walk up the field, beside a wall on your left and climb another step stile into the lane at the top. Turn right and follow the metalled lane for quite a way, ignoring stiles and tracks off it until, towards the end of a stretch where wild gooseberry bushes and trees line the right-hand side you come to a clear fork. Take the right-hand fork and continue down a rough track.

The track winds down passing near to a house on the left. Suddenly a delightful view of Beresford Dale is revealed with the River Dove winding through it. Below the track can be seen a limestone cliff with several caves in it. At a cross-roads of tracks turn left and descend to the river close by a foot-bridge at the entrance to the narrower Wolfscote Dale. Don't cross the bridge but turn right over a small stream and walk beside the river through the open Beresford Dale. Here in the 17th century lived Charles Cotton, in the now demolished Beresford Hall, who together with his friend Izaak Walton wrote the great fishing classic 'The Compleat Angler'. Their praise of the Dove as a trout river is still appropriate today.

At the end of the dale cross the river via a wooden foot-bridge (or the stepping stones!) and turn right to continue alongside the river, passing several weirs before reaching another foot-bridge. Just before the bridge is a deep pool, known as the Pike Pool, in which is a free-standing pinnacle of rock. The pool was a favourite fishing spot of Cotton and Walton. Cross the bridge and turn left to walk now on the opposite bank of the river. After passing four weirs the path leaves the river and climbs gently through the trees to emerge into a field by way of a squeezer or a step stile side by side.

Looking back towards the river you can see among the trees the fishing lodge used by Cotton and Walton. The well-worn path now continues across the fields. It descends to a squeezer stile beside which a tiny stream usually runs. Through the stile bear slightly right up the field, passing close to a post and over the shoulder of the hill to find a stile some way above a gate in the wall ahead. Go through the stile, across a track and through the stile opposite. Continue with a wall and then some buildings on the left. The path reaches a metal gate which leads down some steps between buildings and on to the road. Just to the right the former village garage is now a pottery, specialising in terracotta garden ware, which you can see in production.

Turn right and it is a short distance back to the centre of Hartington.

Some local places of interest: Arbor Low; Hartington village.

13.   Hathersage

An easy route up the quiet valley between the pleasant village of Hathersage and the steep rocks of Stanage Edge.
Distance: About 3 miles (5kms).
Parking: In the car park at Hathersage Church. Map reference 234818.

THE WALK starts at Hathersage Church beside which is a house called the Old Vicarage. Here, in 1845, Charlotte Bronte stayed with her friend Ellen Nussey, the vicar's daughter. Hathersage and its surrounding area made such an impression on her that many descriptions in her novel 'Jane Eyre' fit buildings and places in the vicinity of the village. Hathersage itself is widely accepted as the 'Morton' of the novel.

Start back along the lane which brought you into the car park. At the sharp right-hand bend in the lane a sign on the left beside a stile marks a footpath. Walk a little way along this path to where, beside a large tree, some worn steps lead down into the field on the left. Cross the small clapper bridge over the stream at the bottom and continue forward up the field at the other side, with a fence on your left. The path is not very clear but as you approach the top of the hill bear right and find the wooden posts which form a stile through the wire fence which crosses the field. From here there are very pleasant views back to the church and over Hathersage towards Shatton Moor. Again bear right along a distinct path towards a line of trees at the top of the field. Here you gain a level grassy track which takes you over a wooden stile.

Now keep straight ahead with bushes and a fence on the left until you reach a farm. At this point, looking ahead, you get a first view of North Lees Hall. This is generally agreed to be the 'Thornfield Hall' of 'Jane Eyre' — 'three storeys high, of proportions not vast, though considerable . . . battlements round the top gave it a picturesque look'. Go through the gate into the farmyard and immediately turn right around the top side of the farm buildings to a small wooden gate. From here the path keeps roughly parallel to the farm drive but a little way above it. When a larch tree is reached, just before the drive crosses a stream, the path goes away from the drive along a level grassy track to a ladder stile on to a metalled road. Turn left down the road, passing the entrance to a camp-site, to where the driveway to North Lees Hall goes off to the right, along which a footpath to Stanage is signposted.

Follow the drive uphill, past the Hall and where it bends round behind the Hall go up some steps on the right, as indicated by the footpath sign. The path goes through a gate on to open ground. Continue forward, gradually getting closer to a wall on your right. Cross a step stile into the trees ahead and follow the wide track up to

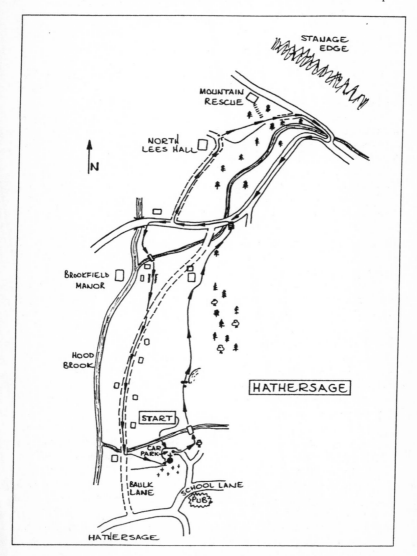

the metalled road below Stanage Edge. The impressive rocks of the gritstone edge are a favourite place for climbers and hang-gliders. There are over 500 climbing routes and it was here that the pastime originated in the 1890s.

Turn right and walk along the road to a road junction. Here turn sharp right again. Continue down the road, passing the driveway to North Lees Hall that you followed earlier in the walk. After passing a house on your right, look for a footpath sign beside a gate on the left, just before the road crosses a bridge. Go through the gate and follow the path towards Brookfield Manor. On approaching a gate marked 'Private' the path bears left, crosses a small stream and passes to the left of an old house. It now becomes narrower and enclosed until a squeezer stile takes you on to open ground again.

Go straight ahead and the path joins a farm track. Turn right and walk along the track, passing several houses on the left. When you reach a house on the right, just after crossing a small stream, climb a step stile in the wall on the left and aim diagonally up across the field to reach a stile at the far corner. The stile takes you on to a path which leads you along the side of the burial ground and into the churchyard. The path to the left of the church takes you back to the car park.

Some local places of interest: Hathersage village.

14.   **Hathersage Moor**

A bracing walk including three small 'peaks' and giving fine views over the heather and gritstone outcrops above Hathersage.
Distance: About 3 miles (5kms).
Parking: The 'Surprise View' car park beside the A625 above Hathersage. Map reference 252801.

CROSS the stile beside the footpath sign at the side of the car park and climb the path straight ahead up the rock-strewn hillside. Keep to the right of the disused quarry near the top. There are numerous examples of partly finished millstones amongst the boulders. These are relics of a bygone industry of this region, when millstones and grindwheels made from the local 'millstone' grit were in great demand. The stones were cut and shaped up on the hills before being transported, often by rolling in pairs, to their destination.

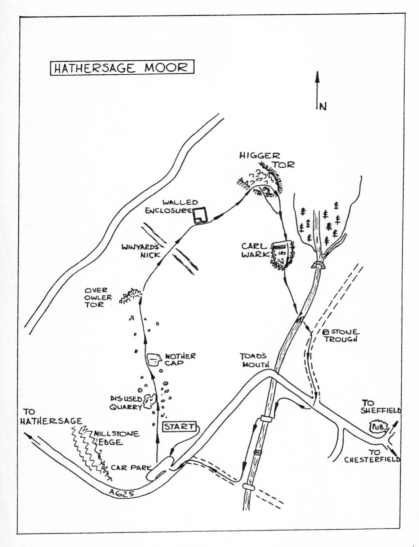

Bear to the left, making for the enormous rock known as Mother Cap when it comes into view. The rocks up here show fantastic signs of weathering — look out for the tortoise! The views are superb — back over Longshaw and Burbage Rocks and forward up the Hope Valley to Mam Tor.

Continue forward to the next large group of rocks, called Over

41

Owler Tor. The path curves to the right at the base of the rocks and then continues, very clearly, through the heather of the ridge to Winyard Nick. This dip in the ground shows evidence, in the form of 'holloways' on either side, of being the point at which old tracks crossed the rocky edge at an easy spot. The path now continues ahead towards the rocky height of Higger Tor. It bears gradually right to reach the corner of a walled enclosure used for penning sheep when necessary. Walk alongside it, with the wall of one of the short sides on your left, to the next corner. Now the path aims straight across to Higger Tor, the way up being clearly visible.

At the top turn right and walk along the flat top of the Tor to where the rocky edges on either side meet. Many of the huge rocks seem precariously poised and are weathered into weird shapes. At the end of the plateau look for a narrow path between the rocks (ignore one which descends not far from where you reached the top). It is fairly easy to scramble down a few feet on to a much clearer path below. The path now makes towards Carl Wark, another rocky out-crop ahead.

Here the path climbs on to the top of what was an Iron Age fort. It is obvious why the site was chosen — clear views all round and steep rocky walls on three sides. The path enters the fort to the left of a bank and wall which were constructed to defend the fourth side. Continue forward along the left-hand edge of the plateau, which gives views to a narrow pack-horse bridge over the Burbage Brook below. Scramble down a narrow path between the rocks at the far end of the plateau to gain a wide and obvious path which takes you downhill to cross the Burbage Brook. Continue up the other side to reach a level track close to where a partly made circular stone trough lies discarded. Turn right along the track, go through a gate and reach the road.

Go through a small gate beside the National Trust sign on the opposite side of the road. Turn immediately right down a grassy path — after a little way a small stream appears on your right. When the Burbage Brook comes into view below turn left to follow it downstream to a wooden footbridge. Cross the bridge, turn left and walk beside the stream. This is a delightful place to paddle in the summer. A little way beyond a small weir a wooden plank bridge is reached. Here turn right up a deep track. This was an old sled route down which millstones from the quarries above were 'sledged' — easier than using wheeled carts over the rough ground. It brings you back to the road almost opposite the car park.

Some local places of interest: Hathersage village; Longshaw Lodge; Padley Chapel.

15.   **Monsal Dale**

A popular riverside walk is part of this slightly more strenuous route which also gives dramatic views from the hills above one of Derbyshire's most picturesque dales.
Distance: 3 miles (5kms).
Parking: In the public car park at Monsal Head. Map reference 185715.

GO THROUGH the lower of the two stiles in the wall at the top of the road leading from Monsal Head down into the dale. Descend the steep path to the valley bottom, ignoring the path leading off to the left part way down. At the bottom near the garden wall of the farmhouse there are large patches of snowdrops in springtime. Turn left around the end of the farm buildings and follow the track to the

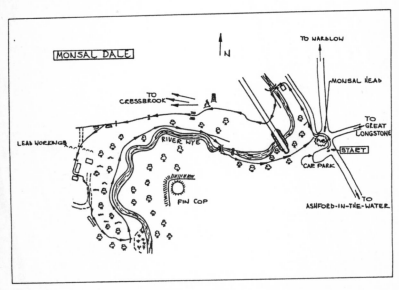

foot-bridge across the River Wye. Over the bridge turn left and almost immediately bear right up a path, through a gate and on to an old railway line. This was the former Bakewell-Buxton branch of the London Midland Railway and when constructed was considered by early 'conservationists' to have totally destroyed the beauty and peace of the dale. However, now the trains have gone, the viaduct adds a touch of drama to the valley and long stretches of the line have become public pathways. The route of the walk continues through the gate opposite but before proceeding it is worth exploring the impressive viaduct spanning the river.

Go through the second gate, turn right and climb the green lane up the hill. The lane, which starts off between two walls, is quite distinct and easily followed. As you climb the hill the derelict chimney of the old Putwell Hill lead mine comes into view over the wall on your right. The chimney is one of the very few remaining on the site of a lead mine in Derbyshire and was constructed for what was thought to be the only underground steam engine in the county. The view gradually becomes more and more impressive. The village of Cressbrook with its elegant old mill can be seen ahead while Longstone Edge and the Hunting Tower above Chatsworth House can be seen behind.

The track eventually curves clearly to the left before continuing straight ahead between two walls and along the edge of the dale, giving stunning views of the river twisting below. On the opposite side of the valley is the extremely steep and bare hillside of Fin Cop, on top of which are the remains of an Iron Age fort and settlement. The views of Fin Cop from this walk make it obvious why the site was chosen, considering the need for secure defences and a good view of the surrounding area.

The path goes through a stile beside a gate and then over a step stile. Almost immediately after this, go through a wide gap in the wall on the left and cross the field bearing slightly to the right to reach a gateway almost opposite. Continue forward through the gateway towards the farm at Brushfield Hough. The bumps and hollows across the field mark the line of an old lead 'rake' which continues over the wall on the left. The wall itself, typical of the limestone walls in this area, contains numerous fossils, the remains of the tiny creatures living beneath the sea which covered this region millions of years ago.

Go through a gate and alongside a very long barn, at the end of which the path turns left into the farmyard. Across the yard turn right through a gate, cross a small field and go through another gate on to the farm driveway. Continue forward to where the drive begins to bend sharply right. Do not turn right but at this point look for a step-stile over the wall on your left.

Climb the stile and bear right. When the grassy path reaches the remains of a wall it turns suddenly left, becoming stony, and begins to descend. It is steep and twisting but quite clearly defined through scrub and small trees, eventually reaching a footpath signpost at the bottom of the dale. Here turn left along the path signposted Monsal Dale.

The path follows the river upstream through the dale, sometimes close to the water, sometimes a little way from it. Trout are much in evidence in early summer, jumping for insects. A little way along the remains of a small water-wheel can be seen at the edge of the river. We have seen crayfish, the freshwater lobster, at this point, an indication of the purity of the water.

Continue to where the path descends slightly, leaving the trees and going towards a foot-bridge across the river, just downstream of a weir. Cross the bridge, turn left and continue along an obvious path which keeps close to the river as far as the weir. Here the clear path begins to climb through the woods to emerge eventually onto the road at Monsal Head.

Some local places of interest: Ashford-in-the-Water; Bakewell; Magpie Mine; Monsal Head Craft Centre.

A nice walk. (a very windy day it blew Grandma's hat off.

16. Over Haddon and Lathkill Dale

One of Derbyshire's most beautiful and interesting limestone dales seen from alongside the River Lathkill and from a hillside above it.
Distance: Just over 1½ miles (2½kms).
Parking: Over Haddon car park. Map reference 203664.

TURN RIGHT out of the car park and descend the steep and winding lane into the dale. Ignore the right turn when almost at the bottom and reach the ford and foot-bridge beside Lathkill Lodge. At this point the river bed is often dry in summer as the water disppears into the limestone bed a little way upstream. If it were not for the bridge it would, in dry spells, be difficult to visualise that water is ever there! However in winter the river is wide and flows swiftly across the ford and beneath the bridge. The old building on the right, upstream of the bridge, is the former Over Haddon Mill. A water-powered mill existed here from at least 1528.

Turn left on the path, along the edge of the river, signposted to Conksbury. After a short distance the path begins to climb the river bank. At this point, in summer, the water reappears from beneath the 'tufa' — the hardened lime deposits on the river bed. Follow the obvious path up the bank, along a level stretch and gradually down again to the riverside. This stretch of the River Lathkill, with its clear trout pools and wooded banks, is a most delightful stretch of water, a beautiful dale in any season of the year. In his writing the famous seventeenth century angler Charles Cotton described the Lathkill as 'by many degrees the purest and most transparent stream that I ever saw either at home or abroad and breeds it is said the reddest and best trout in England'. His description is probably just as appropriate today.

As you continue beside the river you can see evidence of the disturbance of the ground from the many old leadmines on the slopes on the left. There was even a local 'Klondike' gold rush in 1854 when gold was thought to be present in a lead mine. The £1 shares in the Over Haddon Gold and Silver Mine reached £30 each but within two years the excitement had died down and the company was no more. Accounts vary of why this was so. One suggestion was that the gold was present in such small quantities as to be uneconomic to mine while another says that the 'gold' was only iron pyrites or 'fools' gold'.

The path eventually emerges on to a tarmacked road at Conksbury Bridge. Turn left to ascend the road to the sharp right-hand bend part way up the hill. Go through a stone squeezer stile in the wall on the left and climb the short steep path to another similar stile which leads into a field just below the brow of the hill. Turn left and walk close to the edge of the field to reach another squeezer stile which soon brings you to the top of the dale. From here there is a magnificent view of the part of Lathkill Dale through which you have just walked and across the countryside to Youlgreave. Also revealed are the former trout rearing pools alongside the river which are totally hidden by the vegetation at river level. The long narrow 'island' just above Conksbury Bridge was built in the 1930s to try and improve the flow of this section of the river to suit the trout and grayling. The island together with the trout pools and numerous weirs are attempts over many years to manage the river for the benefit of anglers.

Continue along the top of the dale with a fence on your right until just after the crossing the remains of a wall the path turns right and crosses a stile in the fence. Over the stile keep parallel to the fence for a short way then bear slightly right across the field making for the post of a footpath sign whch marks the position of the next stile in the wall ahead. Once over this stile the path bears slightly right and makes for the white building of the Lathkill Hotel where it emerges into the lane by means of a stile in the corner of the wall. The solitary tree at the top of this final field is an old and weathered Wych-elm with a hollowed trunk which children enjoy exploring.

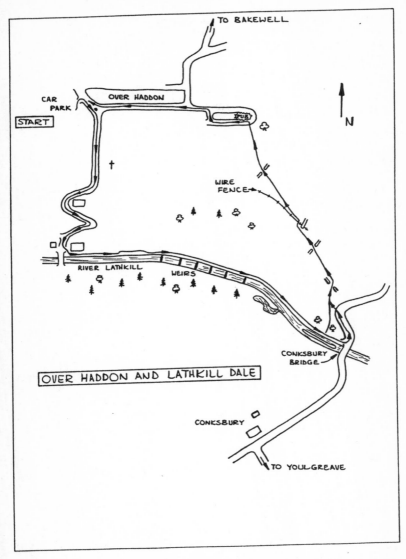

TO BAKEWELL

CAR PARK

OVER HADDON

START

PUB

N

WIRE FENCE

RIVER LATHKILL

WEIRS

OVER HADDON AND LATHKILL DALE

CONKSBURY BRIDGE

CONKSBURY

TO YOULGREAVE

Follow the lane through Over Haddon, a typical village of the limestone plateau, back to the car park.

Some local places of interest: Arbor Low; Ashford-in-the-Water; Bakewell; Haddon Hall; Youlgreave.

17. Stanton Moor

A short but interesting walk over a heather-covered gritstone plateau which gives extensive views and shows signs of use over thousands of years.
Distance: Just under 2½ miles (4kms).
Parking: Where the steep road from Stanton-in-the-Peak to Birchover levels out at the edge of the village there is a small lay-by on the left. Map reference 243638.

GO BACK down the hill and turn right, just past a post-box in the wall on the right, along a road signposted to Stanton Lees. Walk up the road and where it levels out go through a stone stile beside the second gate on the right. The way is indicated by a footpath sign. The obvious track crosses the fields, over two more stone stiles and continues into the trees with a wire fence on the right. Ignore a wooden stile over the fence and carry on to climb another stile beside a gate. Keep straight on to where the path forks. The left-hand path makes towards another wooden stile over a fence. However keep to the right-hand track and you will very soon see the Nine Ladies stone circle to the right among the trees, with the King Stone a little way beyond.

After investigating the Bronze Age stone circle, which is some 35ft. in diameter and is thought to have been of importance in ritual and worship from about 1500 BC, return to the main track. A grassy path leads off to the left almost opposite the stone circle. If you look in the direction in which this path runs you will soon see the Reform Tower a little distance ahead through the trees. Make towards this. The path, which leads to the Reform Tower, becomes worn and very distinct after a little way. The Reform Tower was built by Earl Grey in 1832 to commemorate the First Reform (of Parliament) Bill.

From there the clear path continues, bearing right across the moor. Stanton Moor contains many Bronze Age burial chambers, long ago investigated and disturbed by amateur antiquarians. Most appear as slight mounds strewn with half-buried stones and with a slight depression in the centre. Continue along the obvious path, from which on a clear day the unmistakable outlines of Riber Castle and Crich Stand can be seen far to the left. The path later becomes grass-covered and when a large clump of rhododendrons appears ahead, ignore another grassy track to the left and keep straight on, passing to the right of the rhododendrons. Just beyond these the

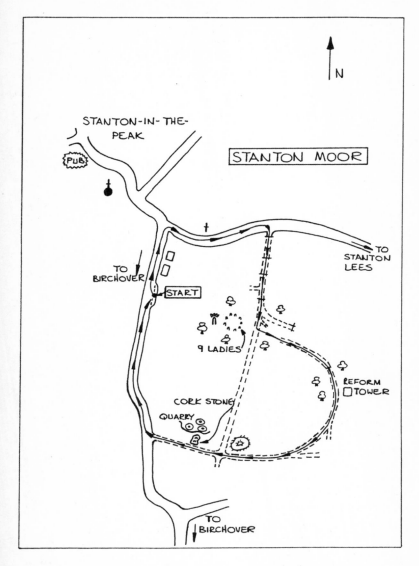

path joins another more distinct path and continues straight ahead. The path soon crosses another and there is a very fine example of a burial chamber on your right at this point.

Go straight ahead at the 'crossroads' and over the brow of the hill you will find the Cork Stone. This curious solitary stone has at some time in the past had footholds cut into it and iron handgrips fixed alongside them to make it easy to climb. If you approach very carefully to the edge of the disused quarry behind the Cork Stone you can see several millstones lying in the bottom, at varying stages of completion. (For further details of millstone production see the Hathersage Moor walk). The clear track now takes you over a stile beside a gate and on to a quiet road. Turn right and walk along the road, from which there are particularly fine views, back to the starting point.

Some local places of interest: Caudwell's Mill; Haddon Hall; Red House Stables Carriage Museum; Rowtor Rocks; Winster.

18.   Tissington

1 - 4 - 90   1½ hrs

This easy route along a former railway line gives extensive views over peaceful countryside before returning through the village.
Distance: About 3 miles (5kms).
Parking: Tissington car park. Map reference 178521.

TISSINGTON is a very attractive and unspoilt model village in a delightful setting. The Derbyshire custom of well-dressing is thought to have originated in the village as long ago as 1350 and villagers still dress five wells at Ascensiontide every year. Its Jacobean hall, built in 1609 by the Fitzherbert family, is still occupied by them. The church has features dating back to Norman times, particularly the font and the carvings around the doorway.

The walk starts from the car park situated where Tissington station formerly stood, beside what was the old LNWR route from Ashbourne to Buxton. Regular passenger services ceased in 1954 and the line finally closed in 1967. The Peak Park Planning Board purchased the line, converted it into a pedestrian way with picnic sites and car parks where the former stations stood and opened it to the public as the Tissington Trail in 1971. Several other former railway lines in Derbyshire have been similarly converted. Some interesting pieces of railway 'furniture' can still be found beside the trail and the cuttings and embankments have become a haven for wildlife. A great variety of birds, flowers, trees and bushes are to be seen and the rocky sides of cuttings, where the line was blasted through, are often dotted with striped grove snails in a variety of colours.

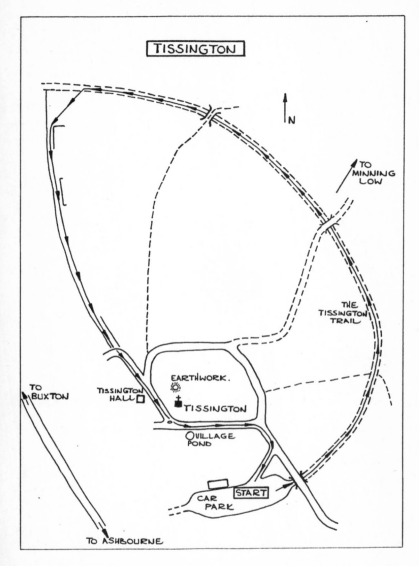

Go under the bridge at the end of the car park and walk along the bed of the old railway line. The way alternates between cuttings and embankments, the latter giving very fine views over the Bletch Brook towards Parwich. The furthest hill top, crowned by a small clump of trees, is Minninglow, the site of a large neolithic burial chamber and is a prominent local landmark. A gradient sign and a mile-post from the old railway can be seen beside the trail.

After passing under two more bridges, at the end of a shallow cutting, you find footpaths lead off on both sides of the trail, right to Parwich and left to Tissington. Climb the stile on the left and bear slightly right across a large field. At the far right-hand corner a walled track leads off. Follow this clearly defined track — sometimes walled, sometimes open — across the fields towards Tissington. The final walled stretch takes you on to a metalled road at a sharp bend.

Continue along the road in the same direction and into the village. On the left, at the first road junction, is the Hands Well. Walk down the main street passing Tissington Hall on your right and Hall Well on the left. At the bottom of the street the building opposite is the old school. Turn left here to pass the village pond on your right and then Town Well on your left. Keep straight on at the road junction and just around the bend is the entrance to the car park.

Some local places of interest: Ashbourne; Tissington Church.

19.   Win Hill

This walk is included simply for the wonderful views obtained from the summit of Win Hill. It is probably the most strenuous in the book but is very well worth the effort. Walking boots or wellies are a must as one short stretch is often very muddy.
Distance: Around 2½ miles (4kms).
Parking: On the roadside at Aston. Map reference 185839.
(To reach Aston turn off the A625 between Hope and Hathersage up the narrow lane signposted 'Aston only').

WALK DOWNHILL along the deeply hollowed Aston Lane. In spring the high banks, down which numerous small streams tumble, are bright with celandines and violets. Pass a barn on the left and shortly beyond a right-hand bend, where the view opens up to the left, turn right up a farm lane with a public bridle-way sign for Win Hill. Where the lane turns sharp right to Edge Farm turn left to continue up a now much rougher track signposted to Hope Cross. This next section can be very muddy, particularly in winter.

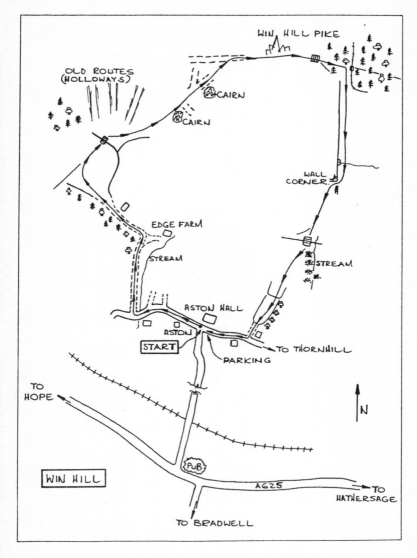

The track passes through two gates to eventually open out into a field. Here turn right and climb the field to a ladder stile at the top. Over the stile bear right and follow the path uphill, past a cairn and on to the open top of the hill. You can see the peak of Win Hill ahead. Keep on a slightly right-hand course to pass a second cairn and join another obvious path which runs along the top of the ridge. Now the view to the other side of Win Hill is suddenly revealed. Below lies Ladybower Reservoir, with the Woodlands Valley and an expanse of moorland beyond.

Turn right along the path to the rocky knoll which marks the summit of Win Hill. The 1516 ft. Win Hill commands extensive views of the surrounding area and is said to be the site of the camp of Edwin, King of Northumbria, prior to a battle in the Hope Valley. Edwin won the battle and legend has it that the hill then became known as 'Win' Hill. The nearby hill on which his defeated opponent prepared for battle was thereafter known as 'Lose' Hill. Descend the clear path on the further side of the knoll to a ladder stile over a wall. Avoid the grassy path which goes off slightly to the right and follow the stony path over the brow of the hill and down through some trees.

When a wire fence is reached at the top of a dense plantation ignore the wooden stile over it and turn right to follow a pleasant grassy track along the contour of the hill with a wall on the right. Below, in the valley, is Yorkshire Bridge formerly on the boundary between Derbyshire and Yorkshire. The modern houses were built to re-house the residents of the villages of Ashopton and Derwent which were submerged when the Ladybower reservoir was constructed.

Just after passing a water trough on the right, from which a small stream crosses the path, look for a gap in the wall, just before the main path starts to descend. Go through the gap and bear left along a clear grassy track, which gradually moves away from the wall on the left, becomes deeply hollowed and descends the hillside to a ladder stile.

Over the stile, aim for a wooden step stile at the lower right-hand corner of the field. Cross the stile and continue in the same direction to another step stile beside a gate leading into a walled track which runs behind a house on the left. This takes you back into the road at Aston. Where the track meets the road there are two old stone water troughs which, in spring, seem to be much favoured by frogs for laying their spawn.

Turn right along the road to return to the starting point. The large interesting looking house overlooking the road is Aston Hall, built in 1578.

Some local places of interest: Castleton; Hope; Ladybower Dam.

27th March 1989
Easter Monday.

20. Wormhill and Peter Dale

Starting in the quiet village of Wormhill this easy route goes through a
small limestone gorge and along walled paths above it.
Distance: About 3 miles (5kms).
Parking: On the roadside in front of the church at Wormhill.
  Map reference 124743.

FROM THE CHURCH walk a little further along the lane and just
beyond a house turn left on a walled footpath. On reaching a
footpath sign, after a few steps, turn right over a wooden stile and
into a field. Go straight ahead across the field to another wooden
stile just to the right of a solitary tree. Cross the stile and bear left to
the far corner of the field where a walled track leads off. Follow the
track and at a point where another joins it from the left continue
through a small wooden gate. In summer the cranesbill, scabious,
harebells, bedstraw and many other flowers make this section of the
walk particularly memorable. Follow the track on to the end where
another small wooden gate leads into the open dale below.
Continue ahead to reach the minor road via a stone squeezer stile.
   Turn right and a short distance on, a stile on the left leads into
Monk's Dale Nature Reserve. The path now follows Peter Dale, a
narrow but impressive dale bounded by high limestone crags and
containing a variety of interesting plants. Eventually the path
emerges into another minor road opposite a bungalow. Turn left
and soon, just beyond a building on the left, turn left through a gate.
Bear slightly right and climb a walled track which opens out into a
field above the dale.
   Shortly after passing through some gate-posts, the path gradually
moves away from the wall on the left, crosses a slight dip and passes
to the right of some trees before reaching a gate. Go through the
gate and turn right to follow the wall on your right. Continue ahead
through a second gate to reach a stone step stile in the wall to the
right of a row of trees. Now bear left over the next field to cross a
stile just to the right of a water trough. Follow the wall on your left.
Shortly after crossing a stile beyond a ruined barn the path turns left
over a wooden step stile. Then it turns immediately right to climb a
stone step stile and continues with a wall on the right to the minor
road at the top of the hill.
   Turn right and walk on to the road junction. Here turn left and
follow the road back into Wormhill. Just before you reach the lane
leading to the church you will pass the village stocks and a very
elaborate village well. This well was built as a memorial to James

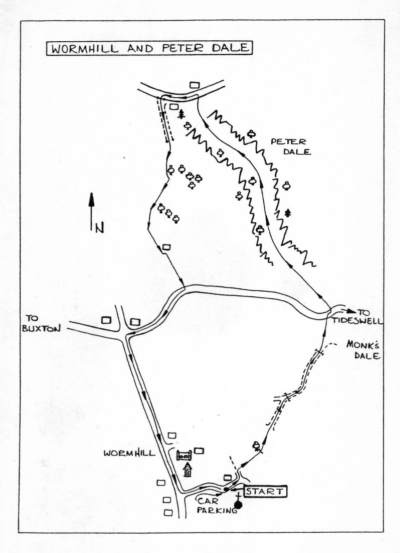

Brindley the renowned 18th century canal engineer who was born in Wormhill. The church has an unusual tower which is more typical of the Rhine area of Germany than of Derbyshire or of England and is said to be modelled on the Saxon tower at Sompting in Sussex.

Some local places of interest: Buxton; Tideswell.